Zach and the Hole in One

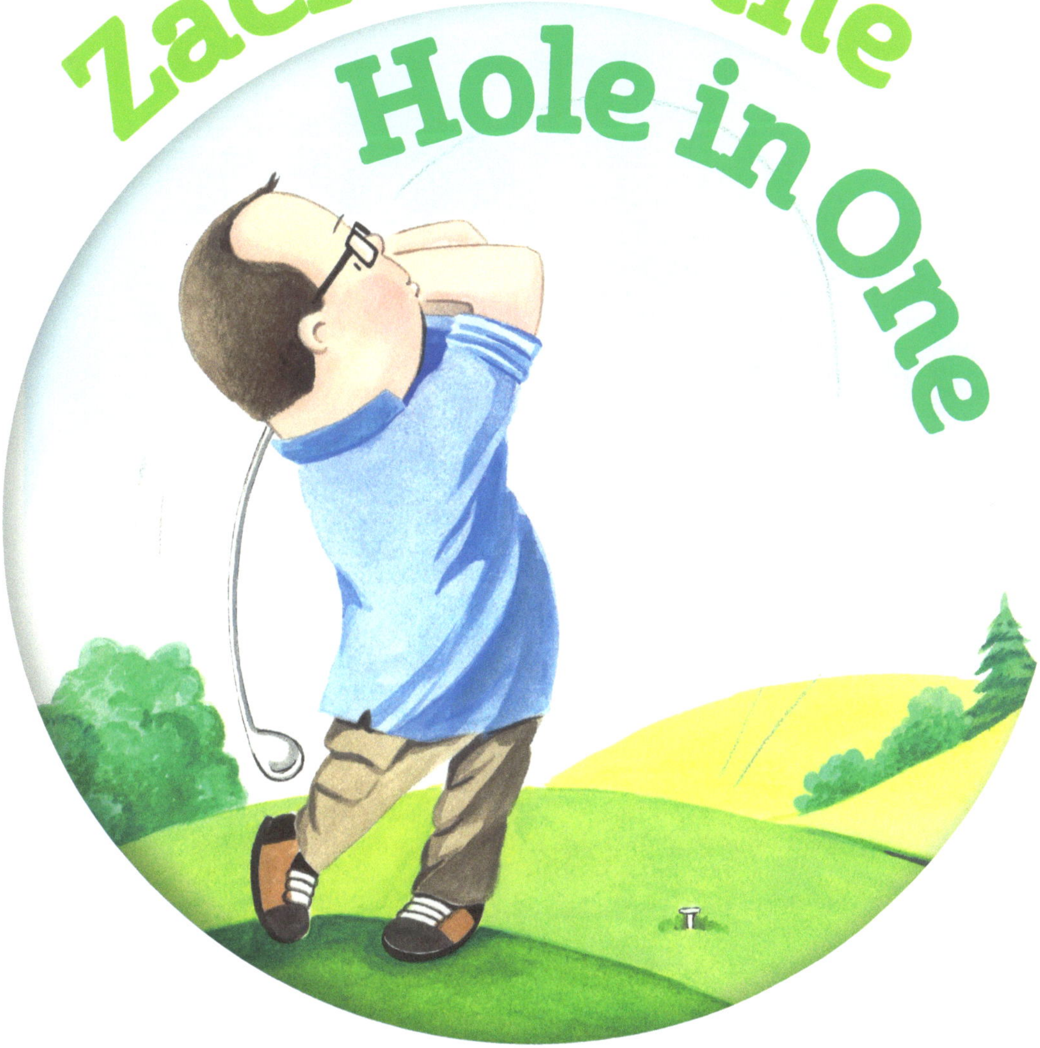

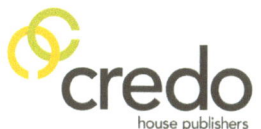

Written by **STEPHEN CHOU**

Illustrated by RACHEL BAINES

credo
house publishers

Zach and the Hole in One
Text copyright © 2022 by Stephen Chou
Illustration copyright © 2022 by Rachel Baines
All rights reserved.

Published in the United States of America by Credo House Publishers
a division of Credo Communications LLC, Grand Rapids, Michigan
credohousepublishers.com

ISBN: 978-1-62586-213-6

Illustrations by Rachel Baines
Interior design and typesetting by Sharon VanLoozenoord
Editing by Donna Huisjen

Printed in the United States of America

First edition

*To Zach Aalderink,
the most life-loving person I know,
and to all those with special needs
who remind us what truly matters in life.*

*To Zach's parents, Rick and Linda Aalderink,
for continuously advocating
for Zach's opportunities
and always seeing Zach's potential,
and to all parents of children with special needs
who work hard to do the same.*

This is Zach, a boy with Down syndrome.
Each of his cells has an extra chromosome.
But being different doesn't stop Zach.
He gives his all, holds nothing back.

Zach wants to share amazing stories,
All of which point straight to God's glory.
This tale is one that's bound to stun.
Let's read about Zach's hole in one!

One day, Zach decided
to try a new sport.
Basketball didn't work,
because he was too short.
Zach loved football,
but he didn't like to run.
What else could he play
to just have some fun?

Grandpa suggested, "Let's give golf a try."
It's all about stance, about clubs, about lie."
Grandpa taught Zach to play the sport with heart.
He even showed Zach how to drive the golf cart!

They first warmed up at the driving range.
Each different club felt new and strange.
Zach's first attempts hissed *whiff* *whiff* *whiff*.
Discouraged, his arms grew more tense and stiff.

Three golf pros nearby swung *whap* *bap* *clap*.
They laughed as Zach missed the ball by a gap.

They practiced next on the putting green.
The golf pros stood bent, and their senses were keen.
They sank their putts with pride and ease.
Zach took his aim but had quivery knees.

His putts went too far . . . too wide . . . too short.
The pros mocked, "You should try a different sport."

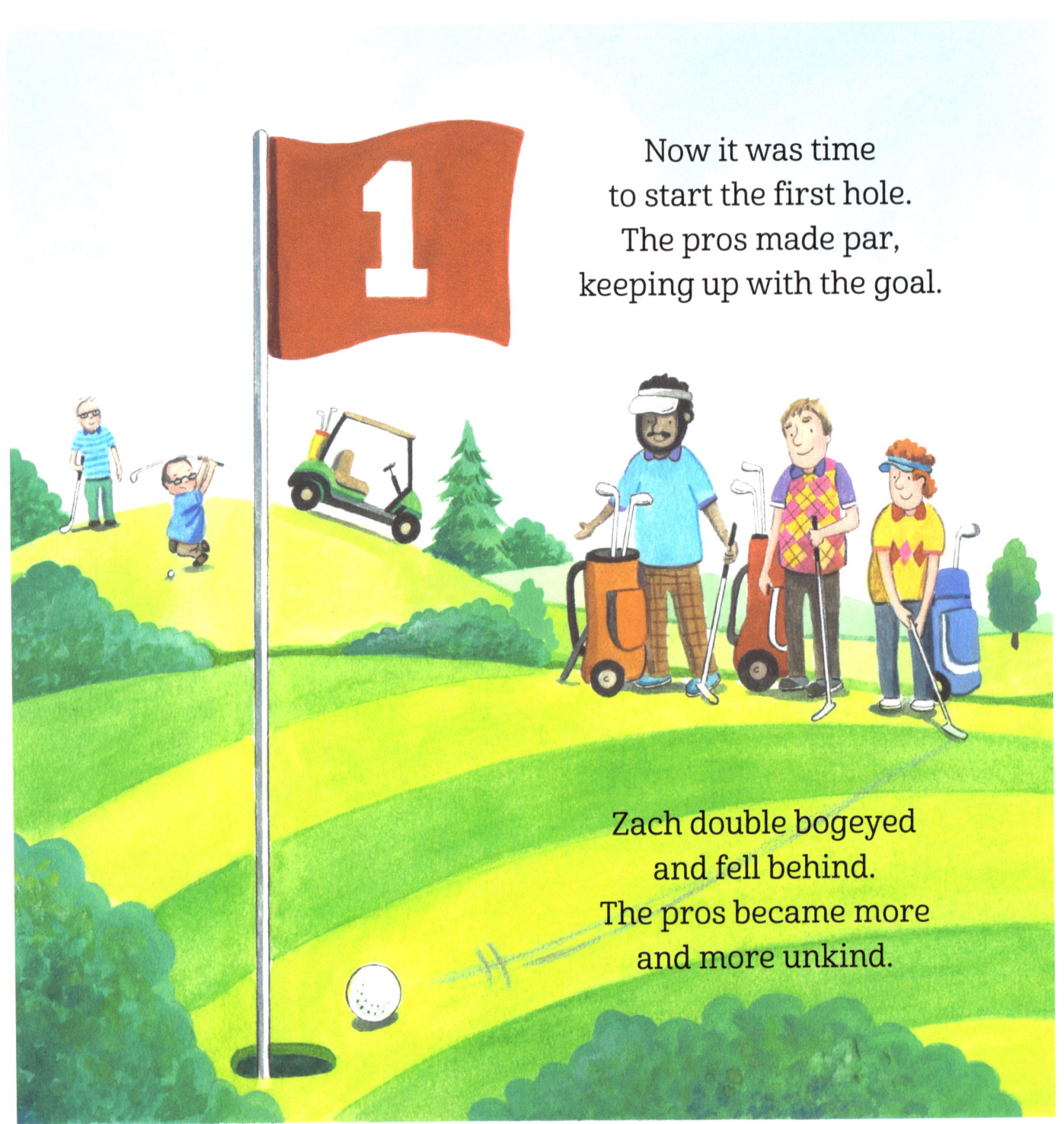

Now it was time
to start the first hole.
The pros made par,
keeping up with the goal.

Zach double bogeyed
and fell behind.
The pros became more
and more unkind.

Finally, they got to the last hole, the nine,
one-twenty-two yards in a l-o-n-g and straight line.
Zach placed his tee and balanced his ball,
then he took his stance in the sight of them all.

Zach lined up his hands, thumb over thumb.

He spread out his feet and stuck out his bum.

He stared at the ball
and smacked his dry lips.

He reared his arms back
and then swung with his hips.

His aim was true
and right on track.
The club smacked the ball
with a mighty CRACK.

Zach watched the ball fly up . . . up . . . up!
It looked like a pebble soaring towards the cup.

The ball reached the green and took a big bounce.
"Nice shot!" a pro was moved to announce.
It bounced once more, this time just past the pin.
The group moved, but Zach stood still with a grin.

"Wait, wait, wait."
Zach held up his hand.
"It's not over yet."
His gaze surveyed the land.

The bounce left the ball
on a slightly sloped knoll,
And look, sure enough,
it had started to roll.
Spinning back toward the hole,
that ball didn't stop.
The crowd, open-mouthed,
could hear the slight plop.

"A HOLE IN ONE!" the audience cheered.
"It's never been done! Not by anyone here!"

The golf pros regretted the mean things they said.
Now they had so many questions instead.
"What is your secret? Your driver? Your shoes?
Tell us about all the things that you use!"

With pride, Zach responded, "It's not about stuff.
I was made by God, and that's more than enough.
I love my life and the awesome things I've done,
and now I can say I've hit a hole in one!"

Zach hit a hole in one in June 2014, 122 yards on hole 9.
He then hit a second hole in one in November 2016, 85 yards on hole 5.
Below are newspaper articles and photos from both events.

Aalderink sinks another hole-in-one

Hamilton's Zach Aalderink hit his second career hole-in-one last week. On the 85-yard fifth tee of Diamond Springs Golf Course, he used a five-wood on the hole. He was out golfing with Hamilton golf head coach Kevin Arnold. Aalderink started golfing in 2013 and now has two hole-in-ones and also has Down Syndrome. Arnold said it is extremely rare for a golfer to have two, hole-in-ones. Aalderink is also the Hope Basketball Manager and Hamilton Football Manager.

www.ingramcontent.com/pod-product-compliance
Lightning Source LLC
Chambersburg PA
CBHW041723040426
42452CB00031B/123